Unbound

Twitter thoughts for the heart and mind

Verlaine-Diane Soobroydoo

Foreword by Resul Pookutty
Oscar Winning Sound Designer, Slumdog Millionaire

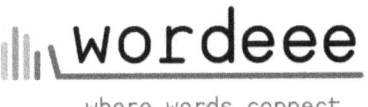

Unbound

Twitter thoughts
for the heart and mind

Unbound Twitter thoughts for the heart and mind

All rights are reserved. No part of this book may be used or reproduced in any manner whatsoever without the copyright owner's written permission except for the use of quotations in book reviews.

New Edition
Copyright © 2021 Verlaine-Diane Soobroydoo
ISBN: 978-1-946274-76-2 (paperback)
ISBN: 978-1-946274-77-9 (eBook)
Library of Congress Control Number: 2021948948

Jacket design: Sarah Messina
Illustration and interior design: Sarah Messina
Author Photograph: Wilson Mbiavanga

Published by Wordeee in the United States Beacon, New York 2021
Website: www.wordeee.com
Twitter: twitter.com/wordeee
Facebook: facebook.com/wordeee
e-mail: contact@wordeee.com

ADVANCE PRAISE

"With *Unbound*, Verlaine-Diane takes us on a journey to discover the freedom within us, regardless of the external circumstances we face on a daily basis. The past two years have been difficult for so many reasons; the uncertainty of the pandemic, sickness, loss, racial and political tension, protests, riots, suffering, war, people being displaced from their homes, separated from their families. Meanwhile, so many of us were locked down, quarantined in our homes, sometimes alone, often feeling helpless and numb watching it all unfold. While the poetry contained in these pages speaks to the times that we are all living through together, the personal lessons being graciously shared are everlasting, and profound. They will continue to live on in the hearts of anyone who reads them, as a reminder to keep going, keep breathing, keep creating, and keep seeking the inner peace that can only be unlocked by becoming *Unbound*."

—**Tennille Amor**, *Singer and Songwriter*

"Everything your heart needed and you didn't know it."

"I have taken daily inspiration from Verlaine-Diane's Twitter feed for some time now and this collection is an incredible extension of what my heart needs to hear, just like her tweets. Not only is it beautifully written, it uplifts my spirits and leaves me feeling empowered, hopeful and grateful. Even while dealing with heavy topics such as what we experienced through 2020, above all, it feels to me like a celebration. I love that I can sit at length to read it all or simply open a page and get what I need and still I put it down completely satisfied! To me this book is creating the positive change that the author builds daily through her words to the world and through her work as the founder of *Zahara's Dream* - she's championing the human experience and hope and connecting us all as a community!"

—**Malia Baker**, *Actress*

"A Celebration of Possibilities!"

"In this beautiful and inspiring book, Verlaine-Diane Soobroydoo celebrates the unlimited possibilities when we open ourselves to loving, encouraging and caring for each other. She takes by the hand—and by the heart - and walks with us in exploring strength in times of adversity, peace in times of turmoil, and love in times of fear. A sweet and rewarding exploration!"

—**Sharon K. D'Agostino,** *Founder SayItForward*

"As I was reading Verlaine's book, I kept thinking what a gift, a treat, the collection of her thoughts and musings is. Culled from twitter and packaged into a beautifully illustrated book, it reminds me of a box chocolates. It is filled with wonders, wisdom, and truths passed down through generations calling on all of us to be: better, kinder, more authentic selves. Like with any box of chocolates, it was temping to finish the entire book in one sitting. But, I'm glad I took the time to sample around different chapters, to savor the messages, the questions, and the tips that Verlaine so generously offered in her writing. At other times I paused to let the bigger truths she was conveying sink in, and to admire her crafty way with words (both in English and French).

I can only hope more people heed Verlaine's call for more compassionate leaders in the world, take the time and share their gratitude with those who made a difference in our lives, and be at peace with ourselves and the world. Verlaine has been doing her part to light up her corner of the internet and kindle thousand little fires in all of us who follow her. I hope that the book will reach hundreds of thousands more people eager to "jump in, fearlessly" and heal our world."

—**Bojan Francuz,** *New York University Center on International Cooperation*

"Whisperers to live again. *Unbound* releases us back to life! This book is for all of us. Coming out of the most challenging year, Verlaine guides us through discovering how to embrace joy and sustain our best selves. I connected with this book so much because as an only child (in my household), solitude was sacred to me. I filled my mind with goals, affirmations, and secrets. *Unbound* is a journalistic feat and global biography of the trinity of stories, prayers, and LIFE!

I love the way she has broken the book up for easy consumption and tells a story of our collective rebirths. Reckoning, Fall, Whole Again, New beginning, Gratitude, etc. It's not a side table book with sharp or witty sayings but a "diary of deep breaths" that prepare us to "make room." With each page turn, we are primed to ask ourselves introspective questions and prepare for:

- Each challenge (These invisible battles cornering you in dark spaces of your spirit-fight them with grace, resilience, and faith. Overcome them find the strength to push forward.
- Each day (I used to be scared to step into who I am)
- And to savor each victory (Trust, you found the power within yourself...and birthing your becoming.

Brava!! *Unbound* tells us of where we have been, where we are going, and to go with grit and grace."

—**Jamia Jowers**, *Director, International Policy and Development - President, Board of Directors Chicago Refugee Coalition*

"Verlaine so beautifully captures the complexity of a soul's sojourn through life, with all its joy, pain, challenges, and triumphs. I found these poems deeply resonant, powerful, and healing—including her decision to take ownership of her voice by publishing her own tweets. I have come away from this book more highly attuned to the songs all human hearts sing."

—**Leta McCollough Seletzky**, *Essayist and Memoirist, Author of The Kneeling Man*

DEDICATION

To the many teachers, formal and informal, starting with my mother, *Marie*, and my father, who contributed to the creation of the being that I am—

to my godfather, *Tonton Pierre*, for the wisdom

to my first teacher, *Annie*, who taught me more than words

to *Matthias* for our enduring friendship

—and to the many beings navigating life in search of their meaning and transformation.

And of course, my appreciation to Jack Dorsey, for giving life to Twitter.

"They will even take away our name: and if we want to keep it, we will have to find in ourselves the strength to do so, to manage somehow so that behind the name something of us, of us as we were, still remains."
—**Primo Levi**, *If This Is a Man*.

"We die. That may be the meaning of life. But we do language. That may be the measure of our lives."
—**Toni Morrison**

CONTENTS

Foreword i

Note to the Reader iii

Reckoning 1

The Fall 5

Ascension 57

Whole Again 143

New Beginning 203

Gratitude 219

The End 226

From French to English 229

About the Author 230

About the Illustrations 231

FOREWORD
by Resul Pookutty
Oscar-Winning Sound Designer, *Slumdog Millionaire*

Our world has been exceptionally challenging on so many fronts for people whether we were in Mumbai, New York, Lagos or somewhere else. We shared a deeply moving, at times enriching and terrifying experience. We have continued to love, stronger but differently, and away from, but for each other. We feared, hoped, and dreamed of a better world each day after. We still continue....

And in this tangled world, what is there other than being in true friendship, in true harmony with the self and with others? We are all in this universal search for familiarity, understanding and belonging. We are all in need to find a shared reflection, one that authenticates our personal experience, "I see you and I see myself in you." I believe that there is a piece of self in each one of us that is resilient and refuses to give up, no matter how dark a moment can be, knowing at its core that a single moment of empathy can heal and push us forward.

I finally found a book that spoke straight to this reality, and to my heart and mind, in a world of "two hundred and forty characters," a book that is really unbound in its essence.

I was amazed to absorb the essence of Verlaine-Diane, the author, someone who experienced and reflected with depth and compassion on the singular experiences we shared during the pandemic: loss, despair, love, pain, passion, fear, worry, hope and above all, unity. I bonded with *Unbound*. Each page, each word and the far-reaching lyrical journey resonated with my spirit. *Unbound* accurately captures many of the experiences I felt but could not necessarily articulate. And when reading, I finally realized, this is a writer who understands me. This is a writer who knows me and dares to soak her readers in love and power for them to be whole again and thrive—which is exactly what our world desperately needs now.

NOTE TO THE READER

As a child, I cherished moments of solitude. I would spend hours, days, weeks, months—writing, editing, drawing, sharing my inner thoughts with an eternal friend: the journal. The journal always welcomed my raw thoughts and creativity. Countless numbers of pages graciously received the inner secrets of a growing heart and mind.

I continued this introspective exercise differently as a young adult, on a public platform: *Twitter*. There is a liberating force when we allow the self to be vulnerable and to connect publicly with other people who are, too, journeying to understand and deliver on the meaning of their lives. Or just *to be* in a world where the simple act of being the *essence* of who we truly are can be revolutionary. I have found that there is a collective catharsis in undertaking this journey of *becoming* together: healing.

After ten years of consuming Twitter, and three years proactively and intentionally sharing my words, thoughts, and experiences, I recognized and valued the testimony these soundbites represented for myself and for the people who received them, particularly during the past year, as our world experienced a pandemic. Twitter allowed many of us to conceptualize being in community with each other virtually and to create a safe space for open discussions despite the distance.

We are still here, in this curious world, *on hold*. We are seemingly suspended in motion, sharing this transformative experience while holding our breath, hoping for our future and our lives.

While rereading my tweets, and especially those of the recent months, I realized that the words about my experiences were witnesses to a personal growth and to fascinating collective interactions. These words were the bearers of hopes, pains and, somehow, when brought together, formed a unique stepping-stone toward liberation. They also, quite unexpectedly, profoundly resonated with others who responded and made me understand that my experiences were, in many respects, *our shared* experiences.

It is with this understanding that I decided to collect some of the tweets and compile them into this book. Despite the intimidating reputation of the English grammar, its structures and rules are often bent in the pages you are going to read: hashtags, hyphens, spaces, bolded texts are recurring throughout this collection, reflecting my creativity as it emerged for tweets, which remain anchored in the microblogging platform where they originally came to life. I have also deliberately included *timeless* tweets without dates, leaving them floating in the space of these pages.

Now, you may ask, *"Why Twitter?"* I dive into Twitter because Twitter is open, free *(somehow)*, compassionate *(when you find your tribe)* and liberating *(when you allow the vulnerability of your voice to come through)*.

Twitter is for the unheard artists who, just like birds, sing their songs accompanying them with hashtags. Twitter is for the women and men who dare to swim against the tide in the often-dangerous rivers of public discussions and authority. Twitter is for the quick minded, the rule benders, who tap into their creativity to connect, share and build their dreams for justice, freedom, individual and collective liberation. Twitter is for the writers who dare to condense their thoughts into 240 characters, or threads *(when more space is needed)*, and go ahead to stand at the crossroads of their inner vulnerability and global human connection, with the audacious hope to build positive change – one word and one mind at a time.

The tweets captured in this collection focus largely on the year 2020, a transformative time for so many. They do not appear in chronological order because our personal growth and becoming do not happen in a clear path forward. Instead, it is a beautiful struggle. We are becoming in different ways, across time, swerving back and forth, transmuting between the past and the present, the individual and the collective. Life is a complex journey toward liberation and fulfillment, and in this journey, language is free, always in movement, evolving with its time and never confined to any barriers. Language is a testimony to our ability to endure some of the most challenging experiences while keeping hope alive. Language, which also holds the power to oppress or liberate, is a witness to our resilience as human beings and to our power to overcome deep pains and suffering when we find the strength within to remember and articulate who we truly are, stand back up and rise higher every time we fall.

This collection reflects my own journey of ascending out of the darkness as a young adult, transpiring in seven parts – a whole depicting growth, completion and completeness, with each fragment incorporating enduring tweets: *Reckoning, The Fall, Ascension, Whole Again, New Beginning, Gratitude, The End.*

As we continue on our own—individual, collective— journeys, I hope that we all find the tools and words *to be* more ourselves and thrive. *Becoming unbound* is a transformational process, and in this process, rituals such as gratitude, love and compassion give meaning in our lives—even if we do not see the larger meaning of these daily rituals in the moment. The transformation happens slowly, as we become more conscious of our inner selves and of the world that surrounds us. In this effort, you will discover tips to *"Becoming Unbound"* that inspired my transformational experience, which I hope will work for you, too.

I invite you to my lyrical journey and to dive into this collection of tweets—*thoughts, affirmations and poetry that saved me*—with an open mind. My hope is that you find musical notes in the texture of the words and let yourself be carried whenever your heart hears and sings them.

Verlaine-Diane

RECKONING

Some stories are
on fire
burning
slowly
growing bigger, faster
—and those stories need to be told
as soon as possible.

In five words, three sentences
or more.
Longer, shorter.
It's up to the writer.

But these stories need to be told
and they need to be told,
now.

12:40 pm · Feb 16, 2021 ·

Darkness has the tightest hold
on us when it's invisible
—set in motion by fear
concealed in our psyche
moving between the lines,
the pages of our lives
silently settling in our bones
our hearts and minds.

*Darkness: you don't like to be talked to,
seen or understood.*

The only way I know how to conjure darkness
is by writing it into light.

10:54 am · Mar 16, 2021 ·

THE FALL

Violence can be as loud as a bullet
and as silent as the wind—*just passing by*.
Feeling it without really hearing it.

12:23 pm · Feb 16, 2020 ·

It has been so dark
so loud
for so long
I can no longer see.

3:07 pm · Feb 21, 2020 ·

The violence was silent

a silent gun, shooting loud bullets—piercing
                               through my heart

                                             my mind

                 the deepest parts of my spirit.

12:23 pm · Feb 1, 2020 ·

How did I get here?
I am standing outside of myself—inert.

Where can I go?
Where can I run to find solace?

Nowhere. I am already home.

12:23 pm· Feb 1, 2020 ·

And in this home, within myself, an intruder is
tearing down
one by one
piece by piece
the being that I am.

There is suffering in the air.

12:23 pm · Feb 1, 2020 ·

Each particle of my being tries to escape
searches for an exit,
a remedy to silence the pain.

There is no way out.

The only exit is within—and for me to reach it—I
must find the strength to shut the intruder out.

12:23 pm · Feb 1, 2020 ·

Here you are, standing by the cliff, about to fall.

The tears.
The pains.
The sorrows.

They found the dark buttons within you
pressed on them so hard, for so long that you forgot
your own name.

You forgot your glory.

And here you are—on the edge of the precipice.

All it would take is the touch of *this* finger pressing on
your shoulder, one last time, for you to

fall
or maybe
to fly

I hope that you remember your glory and find
the power to fly.

10:51 pm · Jan 18, 2020 ·

Folks around are trembling,
their mouths, moving
are telling me *"it's all right"*
but I can see fear in their eyes
and my heart, somehow still strong,
knows there is something wrong.

I am looking in her eyes
adding light tears
to the wind
She volunteers to show me the way
I follow the way
her footsteps
slowly, diligently
to a black hole
to her inner sense of failure
years of disappointment
settled in every part of
her body
flowing through her limbs
her veins
her heart
her mind
a virus that silently infiltrated every part
of her inner sense of self
now, infiltrating every part of mine.

WAR

#Reminder
When you are at war with yourself
you fight the world.

6:02 pm · Dec 11, 2020 ·

What's the point of planting a seed
watering it to fullness
and once the bud appears
suppressing its growth
reaching deep underground
rooting it out
with the intention to kill it?

10:01 am · Jul 14, 2020 ·

Que se passe-t-elle ?

                        Elle n'est plus là.

We just take it for granted
The good and the bad
They say *"that is the way,
the only way"*
and we stay in the way.

2:19 pm · Feb 21, 2021 ·

Where do they go? She asked.
The people we love, when they die,
where do they go?

I couldn't answer.

I fought with
the shadow of someone's ego
I fought with
our negative and dark projections.

Despair.

8:20 am · Feb 21, 2021 ·

Rewind.

8:21 am · Feb 21, 2021 ·

Never fight with
the shadow of someone's ego.
Never fight with
anyone's negative and dark projections.

7:45 am · Feb 12, 2021 ·

You wake up in the morning
open your eyes,
take another breath
– a breath of life,
of hope.

You pull yourself together again
all the pieces that you were
yesterday
– hopeful to continue today.

You get ready, go out.
Still breathing, still smiling.

There comes a dark cloud.

You hear a sound,
your heart skips.
Your heart beats, races.
You know that sound—you know your color.

You know the colors,
the color of fear, the color of guilt.
The assigned colors that may trigger
their fear, their guilt.

So you stop. This is the right thing to do
they said, to stop.

So yes, you stop.

You make a quick call, the call of hope
the call of relief

We all know that call, the call of mom.

You call hoping that your heart will stop racing,
because you know that voice.
the voice of comfort,
the voice of love.

Pause.
Eternal time, eternal love.

Back to reality, back to now.

A sudden move—*whose move?*
So quick, you can't hear,
you can't see.

A loud sound.
It all falls down.

Silence.

And all that remains are the tears,
our tears
our grief
and the breathless body
—your body that woke up this morning

Still breathing
Still standing
Still smiling with the hope to continue.

A hope shattered,
cold body lying down,
deliberately covered by white sheets
lifeless, alone in the streets.

Why?

#DaunteWright

– The Guilt, *whose guilt?*

1:16 pm · Apr 12, 2021 ·

External hate towards others
a shadow
capturing the internal hate towards
the *self*
pains, fears, ignorance
deep-seated dark struggles
rising to the surface
how could his life not mean anything?

There is one reality:
we see, feel and move in the world
as we are.

We honor you #AhmaudArbery

12:58 pm · Feb 23, 2021 ·

The normalization of black death is indescribably painful.

12:53 pm · Oct 27, 2020 ·

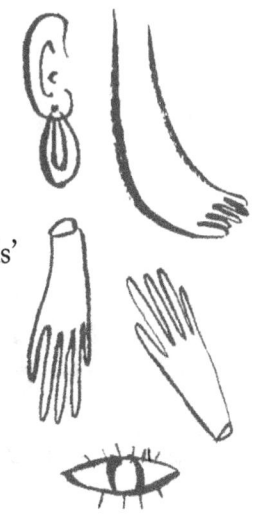

Our society is trained
to transplant people
Deliberately reproducing individuals'
mindsets
ways of being
ways of thinking
Meticulously dissecting
rewiring
what cannot be understood
Body parts removed
beliefs extracted
Transferred from one person
to the other.

They say, *"we're just removing your damaged, diseased cells. We just want to make you better."*

If so, why are you removing my healthy parts?

8:54 am · Nov 19, 2020 ·

I have questions for you:
Who broke your heart, your dreams?
And why are you trying to break mine?

8:35 am · Feb 26, 2021 ·

The world will often tell you what cannot be.
what should not be.

11:47 am · Oct 19, 2020 ·

Prison kills your spirit

There is no laughing.
There is no creativity.
There is no thinking.
There is no writing.
There is no music.
There is no lyric.
There is no you.

Prison, with or without bars, just kills you.

WHAT DOES IT MEAN TO BE WHOLE?
I HAVE BEEN IN PIECES FOR SO LONG.

KILL THE EGO

Can you imagine what the world would look like if all the misplaced egos and prides could be put to rest for a day?

10:25 pm · Nov 28, 2020 ·

BECOMING UNBOUND...

LET GO OF THE EGO

"Detachment is not that you should own nothing, but that nothing should own you."
—Ali ibn Abi Talib

The purpose of the ego is to protect and build walls around the idea we have of ourselves against the perceived attacks of the external world. We wear masks to hide who we truly are when we are uncomfortable with the self or in unsafe environments. The ego also puts other people down by whispering, *"They are not good enough."* The ego judges and discriminates based on a hierarchical model, with the ego at the top and all perceived externalities at the bottom.

Unbound tip: *Take 5 minutes and write down all the attributes you consciously make yours, starting with the sentence "I am...". Include external attributes that may define you (job, titles, ranks, etc.) and internal (compassion, loner, strong, weak, etc.). This requires deep internal reflection. Once done, understand why you attach yourself to such attributes and practice letting go of them in your heart and mind. After detachment, what remains is* you.

Black kid
Inner city joy
Bold dreams
Cosmic inspiration

Dark skin
Long summer night
Chips and water
New friends in town

The word's out there
"work-hard"
grind 'til you reach the stars
the promised seat in the sky

Golden seat
turn up the lights
Box ticked
"We did it, Ma!"

Walked for so long
1,000 steps
For 1,000 days
1,000 times
Rewind

God, I'm tired.
Yes, I'm lost.

What's a golden seat
with a troubled heart
I need to figure out
who we are
all these broken pieces
heavy on my back.

Heavy weight
How did I get here?
How do I reconcile the *selves*
when the weight is not even mine?

These invisible battles
cornering you
in the dark spaces of your spirit
fight them with grace
resilience
and faith.

Overcome them,
find the strength to push forward.

5:34 am · Nov 3, 2020 ·

When the going gets tough,
let the light shine through.

8:08 pm · Apr 7, 2020 ·

Sometimes, you must go backward before you can go forward.

2:08 pm · Feb 24, 2020 ·

Toutes les épreuves de la vie ont un sens—

bien qu'il puisse être difficile de les comprendre à première vue.

2:32 pm · Dec 14, 2020 ·

Our world is on hold.
Our breath is on hold.
We're trying to continue, despite it all.

Just by our experience of the pandemic
—our lives will be different.

8:50 am · Feb 22, 2021 ·

Le temps s'écoule comme de l'eau entre mes doigts, j'essaie de le rattraper mais en vain.

When faced with challenges, you can either
complain
adapt
or
move towards new possibilities.

Choose wisely.

– The Faith in you

7:59 am · Dec 6, 2020 ·

#Reminder
Nothing great and lasting was built in a day
take it one step at a time
to build *you*, too.

1:41 pm · Oct 29, 2020 ·

#Reminder
When things go low
do not go with them.

12:46 pm · Nov 24, 2020 ·

Some, with everything, can't seem to find the strength to give anything.

And many, with nothing, are willing to give everything starting with a smile,
a piece of their sky.

9:11 am · Feb 23, 2021 · Part I

From fullness, fullness rises
From emptiness, emptiness blinds.
                              you blinded me.

9:11 am · Feb 23, 2021 · Part II

You are a walking miracle.
Stop crawling through life.

Stand up.

See: you are still here.

– The Healer in you

2:43 pm · Aug 20, 2020 ·

Our world is hurting.
We are hurting
shattered.

We will have to continue
to find the strength, within ourselves,
to build back up
a different world.

More positive
hopeful
stronger in the sense of things that unite us.

We will build back up
piece by piece
starting with ourselves.

– The Healer in you

11:54 pm · Oct 21, 2020 ·

Don't be scared to start again
flowers bloom on rested and fertile soil.

– The Gardener in you

1:27 pm · Dec 8, 2020 ·

Detach yourself from limits
set by previous experiences
or *thoughts*.

Each new day brings new possibilities,
new opportunities to be and do better.

– The Dreamer in you

3:20 pm · Nov 27, 2020 ·

Never waste a challenge.

Never waste a challenge to learn and to grow even when it's hard.

Challenges allow you to reset and to move towards a new direction.

Learn all you can
and move forward.

4:56 pm · Feb 21, 2021 ·

Learn to enjoy the rainy days
no flower can blossom without rain.

Look: it's raining.

– The planted seed in you

9:16 pm · Dec 17, 2020 ·

There is no guarantee that tomorrow will be easy but we can do our best and try today.

Keep trying
Keep doing
Keep going.

11:34 am · Jul 15, 2020 ·

SURVIVING

Resilience
Adaptation
Imagination
Creativity
Forward

That is what 2020 was all about.

7:56 pm · Dec 30, 2020 ·

Just turn the page.

                    Your next chapter has just begun...

7:12 am · Feb 22, 2021 ·

ASCENSION

Always refuse to be a victim.

> You are more than this.
> Luminous
> Rising beyond the shades
> of darkness.

I see you, beloved,
conquering it all.

2:31 pm · Feb 13, 2021 ·

You get to choose how you respond
to the world around you
and in this response, your energy matters.

When in doubt
choose the response that gives you grace.

– The Healer in you

8:04 am · Feb 24, 2021 ·

How could I remain silent,
and consent to the demise of my*self*?

Hardships give you endurance and resilience.

1:34 am · Jan 30, 2020 ·

Whenever it rains in your life, stay resilient.
Remember that rain gives life.

1:15 pm · Aug 22, 2020 ·

You are not your shadows.
You are more than that.

– The Light in you

12:57 pm · Aug 5, 2020 ·

Allow the truth of your being to come through.

12:13 pm · May 21, 2020 ·

Take a close look at the limitations in your life:

1. When did you decide to set these limitations?
2. Why did you set these limitations?

Now that you have identified these limitations, what are you going to do about them?

7:11 am · Nov 7, 2020 ·

Never rule out a #dream

Be audacious.
Be hopeful.

There is always a possible path.
Find the courage to follow it.
What seem impossible is just a function –
of the moment.

Start now: Paths you never saw before will emerge.

9:15 pm · Feb 17, 2020 ·

Positive change starts with you.

7:26 pm · Jan 31, 2020 ·

Don't feel bad for extracting yourself
from dark places,
places where your light did not belong.

We are vibrational beings.

Sometimes, our frequencies resonate
and melt into harmony.
Sometimes, it's dissonance.

If you're not feeling it, leave it.
Your life and energy matter.

8:57 am · Feb 24, 2021 ·

When faced with challenges
remember that light only enters the cave
through the cracks.

Lean into it

stare at the flaws
touch them
care for them
heal them
bind them with a piece of your golden heart

– The Kintsugi force in you

10:30 am · Dec 18, 2020 ·

When did we start losing time?

Was it when we became conscious of it?
When we realized that time is somehow elusive, just slipping by?

Is time torn?
Can we stitch it up?

Where is it falling?
Can we pull it up?

I look at us, beyond gravity, and know that
time is here and now – in the sound of your melody.

3:28 pm · April 27, 2021 ·

Continuer à avancer par force de conviction.

1:58 pm · Oct 2, 2020 ·

STILL, YOU ARE HERE

I have a thought for you, my friend:

You, who keep standing despite the storms.
You, who keep breathing despite the fears.
You, who keep going despite the challenges
coming your way.

I have a deep thought for you, fighting private battles.

Look, still you are here.

10:45 am · Aug 29, 2020 ·

#Reminder
Transform challenges into a positive force.

3:53 pm · Jun 24, 2020 ·

#Reminder
What is now
is never an indication of what will be.

8:48 am · Feb 23, 2021 ·

#Reminder
Keep faith and keep going.

6:51 pm · May 18, 2020 ·

Embrace your difference.
Embrace your change.

2:36 am · May 4, 2020 ·

Always be in creation
Each voice is unique.
What's your voice?

8:33 am · Apr 28, 2020 ·

Silence is simply not an option.

10:59 am · Jul 13, 2020 ·

You are trying to teach me bondage.
My mother, her mothers and
their mothers taught me liberation.

9:54 am · Feb 25, 2021 ·

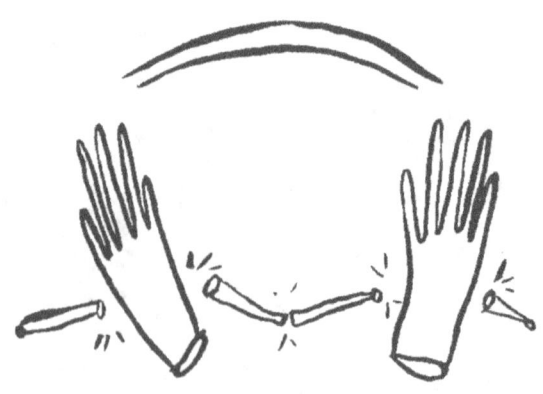

Pay attention to your life.

We are all overwhelmed with distractions,
responsibilities,
movement
and so much more.

Pay attention to your life.
Listen to it.

What does your life need, now?
What would bring joy to this life?

Listen and do.

9:26 am · Feb 24, 2021 ·

Let your greatest pains and challenges
bring your greatest gifts to the world.

2:40 pm · Aug 12, 2020 ·

Remain in creation:
Intellectually
Mentally
Physically
Spiritually.

Wherever you are in your life, trust your process.

This life is a journey.

8:44 am · Apr 27, 2020 ·

#Reminder
Filter your mind.

9:14 am · Nov 24, 2020 ·

Fall a thousand times.
Get back up 1,001 times more.
Let's continue.

– The Dreamer in you

6:10 am · May 9, 2020 ·

BECOMING UNBOUND...

GETTING BACK UP

Falling is a natural part of life—just like rising. Look at nature: the apples fall from the tree, while the tree itself continues to rise and grow despite *(or thanks to)* gravity. You are part of this cycle of life.

Finding the strength to get back up after falling can be tough. Explore the Shaolin philosophy, which focuses on *getting back up* through discipline, respect for life and patience.

Unbound tip: *Take 5 to 10 minutes and write down challenges you faced in the past and how you overcame them. This practice will help you understand the process of persevering through challenges and how to face future ones with confidence and grace.*

It's not about the outcome.

It's about the walk through the darkness.
It's about how you remain open, vulnerable, yet strong.

It's about how the journey unwraps itself.
It's about how you soar despite the fear.

Be gentle with yourself.

– The Faith in You

4:16 pm · Dec 18, 2020 ·

Apprendre à se comprendre

3:22 pm · Jan 28, 2020 ·

Once you stop seeing the other as *other*
but as an integral part of you
you find the strength to meet halfway
your way
their way
new way
to finally rise together

– The Ubuntu in you

7:55 am · Dec 16, 2020 ·

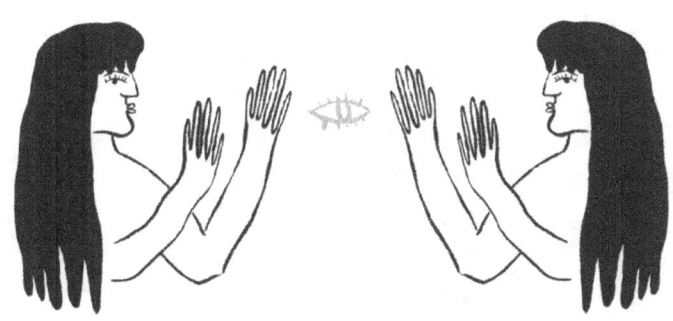

Freedom is understanding that the sun rises for all.

11:18 am · Feb 15, 2020 ·

The love for humanity is the love we need, right now.

3:37 pm · Jun 12, 2020 ·

I hear you want to change the world.
You first have to change your idea of power.

9: 46 pm · Aug 19, 2020 ·

#Reminder
Life has a beautiful way to show you the way.

Follow the way.

9:12 am · Dec 14, 2020 ·

#Reminder
Do not wait for anyone to save you.
You are your miracle.

– The Savior in you

8:53 pm · Dec 11, 2020 ·

BECOMING UNBOUND...

SAVE YOURSELF

We cannot live alone. The sense of community is important to thrive as a human being. We need to nurture that inner strength while leaving space to ask for help. Find a balance: nurture enough of the individual and enough of the community.

***Unbound tip**: Build yourself up, nurture your well-being and, when faced with a challenge, take a moment to determine how you can ensure your well-being and "save yourself" first. Once you have completed this first part, the individual responsibility, ask for help within your community, family, friends, etc. You now complement both parts of the balance: the individual and the collective.*

Why think outside the box?
There is no box.

– The Freedom in you

4:18 pm · Dec 18, 2020 ·

#Reminder: Practice productive persistence.

12:07 pm · Jun 10, 2020 ·

Start small or start big.
But do start.

– The Builder in you

1:00 pm · Dec 3, 2020 ·

Align yourself, your actions
and contributions to the world
with the energy of your being.

7:41 am · Apr 27, 2020 ·

When you get inspired, inspire.
When you learn, share.
When you receive, give back.

9:02 pm · Dec 2, 2019 ·

This generation refuses to live a life of marginalization missed opportunities.

A life of deception.

This generation wants to breathe.
This generation will breathe.

– The Dreamer in you

2:26 pm · May 27, 2020 ·

PURPOSE

For us, purpose is not an option
to be pursued on nights or weekends.

Purpose is everything
and purpose is every day.

– The Dreamer in you

3:38 pm · May 29, 2020 ·

My mother gave me two seeds
a seed for joy
and a seed for pain.

On a warm summer day
the long-forgotten seeds
whispered my name.

My heart heard the song
my body kneeled down,
down to the ground.

I dug.

I dug and buried both seeds.
One so deep, I could feel the earth,
the moist, right under my nails.
The other one, barely covered,
was right up the surface.

Warmth and water
Light and swelling:
Old folks' recipe.

I waited.
I waited for *their* time
I waited
without knowing which of the seeds, *joy or pain*,
would overtake the growth process.

I waited
pressed against the ground
moved by the intertwined feelings
of patience and hurry.

I waited
patiently
for the seeds to rise up
bloom, and bring their glory to this life.

THE PROCESS

It's seldom in the talk.
Sometimes in the results.
Always in the process.

6:53 am · Oct 6, 2020 ·

There is a recipe to build lasting positive change
Community
Love
Intention
Concentrated efforts.

– The Builder in you

8:09 am · Feb 20, 2021 ·

Do the work with
vision
passion
and heart

—particularly when the work involves and impacts others.

Those who will recognize themselves in you will form a union with you

and you
with them.

– The Builder in you

1:32 pm · Dec 3, 2020 ·

#Reminder
Passion
Faith
Grit and resilience will keep you going.

4:38 pm · Oct 2, 2020 ·

There will always be resistance to your growth.
This revolution is not about updating the old system.

It is about redefining the internal structures.

Tabula rasa

This is the creation of a new you.

Accept resistance
transform
rise.

8:50 am · Nov 26, 2020 ·

Maman m'a dit
« Viens, nous allons traverser la vie sans permis, ni billet de train »

3:05 pm · Oct 31, 2020 ·

#Journeying

Sometimes, smooth waters
Sometimes, hurricanes.
We have learned to sail under the sun
and to laugh under the rain.

2:11 pm · Feb 3, 2020 ·

#Reminder
We are done surviving,
we are going to thrive.

9:45 am · Jul 8, 2020 ·

As you start to step into the person who you are becoming
remember that your identity is for you,
and for you alone to decide.

People are going to question it,
misunderstand it
and might even try to take it,
mold it
shape it into a different version of you.

Hold strong to who you know you are.

7:05 am · Mar 23, 2020 ·

Give yourself the space and permission to grow.

If you are looking for answers, just look at nature: with each new season, a new stage is reached.

Why limit yourself?

– The Universe in you

6:31 pm · Apr 13, 2020 ·

#Reminder
Learn to tell your story,
in your own words, the way you are
free from the pen that may write a story
that is not you, that is not yours.

10:57 am· Feb 23, 2021 ·

Really, there is no need to think outside the box when indeed, *there is no box.*

7:50 am · Dec 13, 2020 ·

La liberté fait toujours rêver.

3:08 pm · Oct 31, 2020 ·

#Reminder:
Dream, then do.

– The Dreamer in you

3:03 pm · Dec 22, 2020 ·

Do you remember your first dream?

10:24 am · Jun 26, 2020 ·

It is all about perspective
cultivate all experiences with wisdom
and understanding
even when it's hard.

You simply never know where you will find your growth.

– The Gardener in you

5:09 am · Oct 28, 2020 ·

KARUNĀ

Compassion roots itself
flows
gives back
grows and flourishes for everyone.

We need more compassionate people *leading* our world.
This is what our world needs more now.

– The Leader in you

2:42 pm · Dec 13, 2020 ·

BECOMING UNBOUND...

KARUNĀ: CENTER COMPASSION

Karunā (Sanskrit) translates as compassion and self-compassion. Karunā centers a loving behavior for inner and external well-being. In 2020, we have witnessed how important compassion and loving-kindness are to sustain communities in the face of deep challenges.

***Unbound tip**: Listen to others with an open mind and heart and allow your responses to be rooted in compassion. This means killing the ego, as shown earlier. Be kind, be karunā.*

WOMEN

The voices of the women who
came before us
resonate like echoes under water

their vibrations run through my veins
right under my skin.

Mother
Grandmother
—and her mothers
Where are you?

Women living in us, in you and me
silent in our broken history.
Blurry—I can barely see you.

Agitated voices
soaring from the past
refusing to be silenced
violently emerging within, through and around me.

Take it – my voice is your voice.
My skin is your skin: the untampered memory
of generations rising.

– The Women in us

1:32 pm · Dec 3, 2020 ·

I used to be scared to step into who I am.

*"You are too much. Tone it down.
Women are quiet—*look at *her*, quiet," she said.
"Be like her."

Why?

I just want to be me.
I just want to be *free.*

7:27 am · Jun 25, 2020 ·

"You must write your story, be part of history"
planted seeds,
nurtured seeds,
unshakable roots
of a tree growing
higher, stronger in the heart of a traveler.

– Charnal

I will tell my story.
History is unforgiving to women.

– Herstory in me

3:32 pm · Feb 25, 2021 ·

Take your *power*.
Be visible.

Share your story, in its multitude
of lights
and shadows.

The world needs to hear it
to hear you:
how you fell,
how you rose,
how you survived,
how you thrived.

The past, the present and
the future need your memories.

3:54 pm · Jun 6, 2020 ·

Be like water
move
back and forth
adapt, change: high tide, low tide
swell
take place
retreat
move beyond shape and understanding.

– The Water in you

5:58 pm · Jan 28, 2020 ·

What's her?

The re-making of *Her*story.

6:30 pm · Feb 26, 2021 ·

Espérer. Continuer. Avancer.

Despite all the pains,
the tears
and challenges
Your heart, mind and spirit may have endured
—don't give up.

9:18 am · Jun 23, 2020 ·

No matter how long
or dark the night
the light of day always reclaims ownership of life.

– The Life in you

8:49 am · Apr 30, 2020 ·

There is power in #blackjoy
When you see it
Feel it
Take part in it
Invisible links
Bringing us together
Beyond a world of despair
A world that never expected
the rise of the fallen seeds
Seeds of joy
Joy rooting itself, growing where
hope did not exist.

– to John from V., *two strangers dancing in a curious world*

5:01 pm · Feb 23, 2021 ·

We all have a story to share:
what's your story?

3:57 pm · Mar 10, 2020 ·

You get to shape the space around you.
Change always starts with you,
within you.

There is no good,
no bad time for change.

Start small or big
however you wish
but change always starts with you.

– The Builder in you

5:49 pm · Mar 9, 2020 ·

Before you seek to root out biases and other injustices out of the world, seek to root them out of yourself.

The Journey of learning,
unlearning,
learning again, differently
—is every day.
and it starts with you.

6:49 am · Jun 29, 2020 ·

Never compete with anyone.

Competition rises from the scarcity mindset.
When you are positively full within yourself,
there is no competition.
The only competition is to better yourself
to be a better human being.

Every day.

8:54 am · Feb 24, 2021 ·

Remain hopeful. Remain grateful.

– The Healer in you

5:47 pm · Oct 31, 2020 ·

I chose to give up the work of becoming perfect.
I focus on becoming brave
and simply more myself.

- The Healer in you

« *Si tu souhaites assister au coucher du soleil,
il faut te mettre sur une montagne* »

- Tonton Pierre

Jump in, fearlessly.

8:17 pm · Dec 30, 2019 ·

The future
desired next second.

We are all hoping for this promise
to be fulfilled.

Be here.
Be grateful to be,
to breathe.
Now.

This moment is the gift.

- The Universe in you

11:08 pm · Dec 17, 2020 ·

Let the world

               Reveal itself

               To you.

Turn human disaster into collective triumph.
Purge the trauma:

conjure it all
and let yourself be Whole Again!

- The Life in you

11:25 pm · Mar 26, 2020 ·

WHOLE AGAIN

Silence.

        Silence.

Silence.

        there you are
        silent in the midst of chaos
        the eternal self
        my *self*.

Sometimes, all it takes is to adjust your perspective to see clearer.

- The Visionary in you

7:41 am · Oct 7, 2020 ·

You cannot see the wind,
but it is here,
always present
surrounding you,
protecting you.

10:21 am · Jan 11, 2020 ·

　　　　　　　　　　　　　　The way we move
　　　　　　　　　　　　the way we see
　　　　　　　　　　　　the way we are

in the world
is an expression of our
consciousness.

10:10 am · Feb 13, 2021 ·

I am accepting my light
and my imperfections.

I am owning my power
and my vulnerabilities.

I am shaping my dreams,
and releasing my fears.

I am flourishing in the duality of my being.

- The Dreamer in you

You are the change you have been waiting for.
You always were.
You always will be.

- The Healer in you

10:59 pm · Oct 28, 2020 ·

TRANSMUTE IT ALL

Take action to make a difference
on issues that burn you.

Take action to conjure
the very things that crushed you.

Turn the negative into a positive force
transmute it all
so that other women,
sisters and daughters
do not have to be crushed, too.

- The Woman in you

Your greatness and standing up for what you believe in does not require anyone's permission.

It needs *your* confidence
in *your* voice
and in *your* being.
It needs you.

- The Builder in you

9:47 am · Oct 27, 2020 ·

Do not underestimate your reach
impact and participation in this world
—individually and collectively.

Come with everything that you are,
trusting the voice
strength, and power within you.

7:07 pm · Jul 30, 2019 ·

#WeekendGrowth
Nurture #Positive & #Growth:

✓ Nurturing relationships

✓ Internal grace & energy

✓ Blessings given through you and received

✓ Read, Read, Read

✓ Gratefulness

✓ Distance from anything negative

✓ Care for your body, heart and mind

9:38 am · Feb 29, 2020 ·

#Reminder
You get to determine for yourself
what your boundaries are.

- The Protector in you

1:16 pm · Dec 4, 2020 ·

Why are you trying so hard
to cut the tree on which I stand
from which I tweet?

Don't you know
by now
that I sing *this* song from the depth of my heart
carried by the strength of my wings
with the unshakable belief that I can fly?

6:55 pm · Feb 17, 2021 ·

Fearlessly honor yourself.

5:45 pm · Jul 29, 2019 ·

You cannot silence, a #woman who found her voice
after a life spent in silence
violence and exclusion.

2:40 pm · Dec 13, 2019 ·

I am willing to love you
to appreciate you
from a great distance.

It feels like #AddisAbaba
It feels like #Nairobi
It feels like #Brazzaville
It feels like #Abidjan
It feels like #NewYork
It feels like #Paris
It feels like #Dakar
It feels like #Bamako
It feels like #Niamey
It feels like #Kinshasa
It feels like #Luanda
It feels like #Abuja

It feels like a #Dream in motion.

12:08 pm · Feb 17, 2020 ·

#SELFLOVE

The greater capacity you hold in loving yourself, the better you can love others and give back.

6:57 am · Nov 29, 2020 ·

BECOMING UNBOUND TIP...

SELF-LOVE

Self-love is not contradictory to community and togetherness. Self-love complements them. Communities are made of individuals, with each one contributing to the whole. Imagine how challenging it is for a *broken* piece to integrate fully within a whole; we have all been there, and we know it is hard, if not close to impossible, to give anything when we have little left within us. Heal yourself back to life by centering self-love. You can only give what you have.

Unbound tip: *Take ten minutes and list five main positive attributes you appreciate about yourself (even if you do not practice them yet or fully). Commit to centering them in your life, daily, and witness self-love and positivity take over your life...*

We all have:

✓ The power to listen
✓ The power to speak up
✓ The power the stand up
✓ The power to give
✓ The power to smile
✓ The power to say yes
✓ The power to say no more
✓ The power to act

Now, what will you do with this power?

5:58 am · Jun 6, 2020 ·

Again, we see the world as we are.

- The World is you

10:26 am · Dec 14, 2020 ·

#Reminder
Never mistake what you do for who you are.
You bring who you are to what you do.

- The Life in you

5:56 pm · Dec 18, 2020 ·

SOLAR SYSTEM

The Solar System contains smaller objects.
In these smaller objects, there is Earth.

In this Earth, orbiting around the sun—
there is you.

A living energy within the larger solar system of motion and life.

The Universe.

You are a piece,
a part of a whole.
Keep perspective and be whole in the infinite.

7:12 am · Dec 10, 2020 ·

Today is Tuesday—*and you are enough.*

5:05 pm · Aug 25, 2020 ·

Put love and compassion
at the center of who you are
and what you do.

4:41 pm · Apr 14, 2020 ·

Compassion and empathy: two words
when put into action
can change the world.

9:10 am · Jun 25, 2020 ·

PEACE

When you are at peace with yourself,
your peace builds and heals the world.

- The Peace in you

6:02 pm · Dec 11, 2020 ·

ILLUSIONS

I, too, was conditioned
just like you
and him
and her and them, too

to pursue
food.

Food in all its forms
illusions of riches, skins, and wealth.

Survival in disguise.
Survival state of mind.

Glorified survival
until my skin fell apart.

Until it all fell down
piece by piece
uncovered flesh

Old chains cast off
'til I was light enough
to walk free.

HAPPINESS

Your Happiness is revolutionary.
Let the revolution take root.
Let the revolution bloom.

1:35 pm · Oct 25, 2020 ·

You told me to sit down
Not to move too much
Not to speak too much
Not to be me too much

but *I never really liked* assigned places

So, I stood up
So, I moved
So, I spoke up
So, I decided to be me, fully, powerfully
in the true sense of what the
word free means.

2:49 pm · Mar 2, 2021 ·

Forgiveness, the only payback.
Forgiveness is grace.
Forgiveness is for the *self*.

It is easy to hate, to fear
what we don't understand.

It takes strength to love
It takes strength to understand
It takes strength to include.

It takes strength and a whole *self* to forgive.

4:03 pm · Feb 22, 2021 ·

THREADS OF GOLD

She poured warm threads
of gold
into my hands

Threads running through
my fingers
drops of water
illuminating my soul
nurturing my heart

With these weak fingers of mine
I grabbed the golden threads

one by one

Pulling them
weaving them
tightening them at the center
where the pain had silently settled.

I stared at the wounds
and repeated the process
over and over
precise devotion

I sutured the final knot
bringing *her* back to life.

A life that needed to be stitched back together
A life that needed to be whole again.

9:06 am · Feb 15, 2021 ·

…. Add your magic to the world

- The Bliss in you

10:38 am · Oct 20, 2020 ·

#Reminder
None of us operates alone.
We are all part of a collective: **humanity**.

Honor this reality.

- The Ubuntu in you

7:07 am · Nov 29, 2020 ·

We've got a good grip on each other.
we're talking.

- #HerInMe

Hold on to people
—cherish them, value them—
offer a safe space for exchange and growth.
This is part of our journey.

- The Healer in you

UNBOUND TIP...

APPRECIATION

Cherishing people who surround us is a powerful way to be positive, happy and unbound. Life is relatively short, and circumstances always change. Take a moment to cherish, value and appreciate the people you love.

Unbound tip*: Take 30 minutes to 1 hour to check on your loved ones, family, friends and colleagues to share good news and see how they are doing. Take a moment to share with them how positively they have impacted you by writing thank-you notes or emails at the end of the week, month or year – however comfortable you are with it.*

Remember that
we are all visitors

on track
or not

...for the journey.

Be kind.

- The Visitor in you

7:43 am · Feb 16, 2021 ·

Croire au merveilleux du quotidien.

6:17 pm · Aug 21, 2020 ·

Music
Loyal companion of *my* revolution.

Music
Individual.
personal.
communal.

Music
Social movements
moving back and forth
past and present.

Music
Sound of affirmations,
announcements of what's possible.

Music gives the note.
The note gives the tone.
And the tone gives the much-needed hope.

Music introduces change.

7:43 am · Dec 13, 2020 ·

You know how to fly
you learned it as a child
close your eyes
focus on the sky.

Your mind already flying so high
is carried by your footsteps

Run
Run
Run

Stretch your arms
Deploy your wings

Jump
Jump
Jump

Take off
Higher!
Maneuver, swim in the air
Adjust, steady – rising beyond gravity.

There you are, soaring
already flying so high
part of the sky.

I knew you knew how to fly,
you learned it as a child.

C'est difficile de s'ancrer dans le tout,
quand on a apprécié la beauté du rien.

3:52 pm · Feb 22, 2021 ·

TRANSMUTING

Your journey
of pains
of tears
of sorrows

is your soul's bet to succeed *this time* to transmute all

these pains
these tears
these sorrows

into life, light and possibilities.

- The Healer in you

You get to re-invent and re-define yourself.
Each new day.
Each new breath.
Each moment is yours to be and do—*you*.
Even if *you* is not *their* definition.

- The Life in you

8:54 am · Jan 24, 2020 ·

Reminder: defy expectations

- The Dreamer in you

12:52 am · Oct 7, 2020 ·

Today is the day
when your fragile wings
gain enough strength
to overcome
fear
pains and disappointments
to finally open and fly.

6:37 am · Feb 25, 2021 ·

DIFFERENCE

Never aspire to merge with the material.
Aspire to make a difference.

- The Dreamer in you.

5:25 am · Oct 19, 2020 ·

You are free.

Speak it.
Share it.
Share how you freed yourself.
What are the tips?
The good news?
The bad news?
Help others free themselves, too

- Ode to Toni

12:56 pm · Oct 30, 2020 ·

Self-love feeds you
Self-love feeds others.

- The Love in you

9:32 pm · Dec 17, 2020 ·

Nous avons tous besoin des uns et des autres.

10:58 am · Oct 8, 2020 ·

Once you let love and light take over, you don't want to spend a moment, or dwell in anything that is not love and light.

There is enough darkness in this world.

Be a #lighthouse.

5:18 pm · Feb 17, 2021 ·

#Reminder
You become what you believe.

Make room in your life for the things that matter.
Make room for the things that are to come.
Make room for the present.
Make room for you.

Just make room.

#Reminder
You get to make something out of nothing.
This is called creation.

- The Creator in you

1:00 pm · Oct 23, 2020 ·

Hope
Hope and Life
Hope, Life and Faith.
Hope, Life, Faith
And Laughter

9:12 pm · Mar 24, 2020 ·

There's something about freedom:
words can't fully explain it,
but my whole being knows it.

10:27 pm · Feb 24, 2021 ·

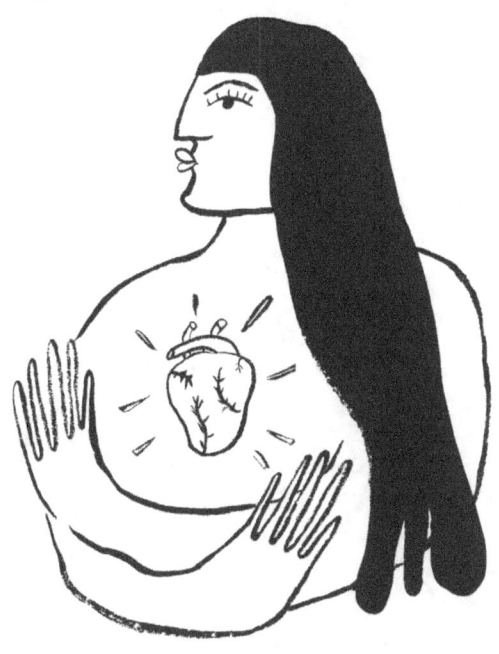

We have work to continue.
It does not stop here.

12:25 pm · Nov 6, 2020 ·

Never limit yourself

                        You are unlimited.

You are the power of your being

The power
of this life

The life before you
The life that is to come

It is all within you.
Tap into it

                        Center it
                  Be it and thrive.

How?

She just persisted.

NEW BEGINNING

Us
being here
is a miracle.

6:27 am · Jul 30, 2020 ·

Good morning: *we are still here.*

Still breathing.
Still standing.
Grace: let's continue.

– The Sun, the Breath, the Heart, the Life in you.

Every morning · Every day ·

BECOMING UNBOUND...

MORNING GRATITUDE

Did you know?

A person dies approximately every 11.14 seconds, while 323 people die per hour, 7,755 per day and 2,830,688 per year in the United States. (Source: United Nations World Population Prospects 2019).

We go to bed every night without the promise of waking up the next day, carried into life by breath. Wake up with gratitude and immerse yourself in the joy of still being here, present, breathing for a new day. You get another chance at life!

Practicing gratitude first thing in the morning clears the personal space for the day and allows you to face challenges that may show up with grace and positivity.

Unbound tip: *Take five minutes sitting to appreciate the new day. If you like to write, note down your gratitude into a journal and your commitments for the day ahead.*

I see you, beloved.

I know it took a long time for you
to get here—to pick up all the pieces
that you were, shattered
on the ground
to find strength
to stand back up
and to carry on.

But you made it, look at you:
Stronger
Better
Wiser

Look back, realize your glory.

10:10 am · Feb 24, 2021 ·

Stare long enough at life
and you will see stars shine bright
in daylight.

7:55 am · Feb 22, 2021 ·

Inhale
Exhale
The breath
Finally, *I breathe.*

4:39 am · Feb 26, 2021 ·

Let your life be a testament to what it means to fall down and to keep standing back up.

1:15 pm · Aug 18, 2020 ·

If you want to go far, go together.

—Prof. Baba, Ibadan.

5:55 am · Nov 5, 2020 ·

Where do they go? She asked.
The people we love, when they die,
where do they go?

They go home, in our hearts, and live in us.

Faith got us here.
Faith will take us forward.
#FaithForward.

4:52 pm · Aug 19, 2020 ·

WE ARE HERE

It took some time for *me* to get here.
We are here:
all the pieces that I am
perfectly imperfect
skillfully wrapped into this being.

A being intentionally defining it*self*
vessel of love
lover of life.

We owe it to our lives to be our definers
the catchers of our experiences
the healers of our hearts
the writers of our stories.

9:41 am · May 11, 2020 ·

It was hard
long
painful
lonely
but I knew
I knew that I could birth
the woman I was becoming.

- The Woman in you

2:18 pm · Mar 14, 2021 ·

Write it like you mean it.

7:50 am · Feb 22, 2021 ·

Writing is therapeutic
when I am writing,
I am healing my body
my heart
and my mind.

9:24 am · Mar 14, 2021 ·

Eternal being
living in me

You fell off the cliff
deep dived: came so close to the ground.

Trust.

You found the power within yourself
to trust
to unwrap your wings
push against the wind
to gloriously fly.

This power was always there
around and with you.

How could I not thank you?

Gratitude

ASANTE

Asante for the good times.
Asante for the bad times.
Asante for the trials.
Asante for the errors.
Asante for the joy.
Asante for the pain.

for the great times and the hard times

have taught us the resilience
to hope
to faith forward
to continue
to grow
and to overcome.

- Asante *Sana.*

2:27 pm · Dec 15, 2020 ·

Remain grateful
for life.
for being.
for this moment.

- The Life in you

1:44 pm · Dec 13, 2020 ·

See, *beloved*
How the world moves,
how time flows
swinging back and forth?

Circling around
spinning our minds
Giving enough time
for the seed of pain and the seed of joy
to meet underground
rise up
and bloom together
melted as one.

You and I are blooming, *too.*

Part of this infinity
but for now, only.

9:10 am · Feb 12, 2021 ·

What are you grateful for today?

Recurring tweet · every evening ·

BECOMING UNBOUND...

EVENING GRATITUDE

They say, *"A grateful heart is a powerful heart."* Gratitude is an energy booster and gives meaning to our lives. By practicing gratitude, we can build positive energy and be present in and appreciative of the moment. Giving thanks for who we are and what we have, starting with *the breath*, is the beginning to happiness.

Unbound tip: Take five minutes at the end of the day to appreciate the strength you carried to overcome challenges you may have faced and to appreciate all the positive things that happened. Take a piece of paper and list three things for which you are grateful for today, even small things. Practicing gratitude at the end of the day re-centers you and allows you to let go of anything that does not serve a higher purpose and positive energy as you prepare to rest, and hopefully, wake up and start as a new person for another day.

We are still here.
Still breathing.
Still standing.

Grace: *we will continue.*

Believe it.

Nothing is eternal,
everything comes to an end.
The body, too, gives itself back to the very earth that nourished it.

Life gives itself back to life.

That is, my friend, endless:
the meaning of *Unbound.*

- The *Unbound* in you

La fin.

N'est-*elle* pas un éternel recommencement?

FROM FRENCH TO ENGLISH

Page 17:   *What is happening? She is gone.*

Page 40:   *All of life's trials have meaning, although it can be difficult to understand it at first glance.*

Page 42:   *Time flows like water between my fingers, I try to catch up to it but to no avail.*

Page 71:   *Let's continue, by the strength of our convictions.*

Page 87:   *Learning to understand each other.*

Page 108: *Mother told me: come on, we'll go through life without a permit or train ticket.*

Page 115: *Freedom is always a dream.*

Page 128: *Hope. Continue. Moving forward.*

Page 138: *If you want to watch the sunset, you have to climb up the mountain.*

Page 181: *Believe in the wonders of everyday life.*

Page 184: *When we have tasted the beauty of emptiness, it's hard to get into everything.*

Page 192: *We all need each other.*

Page 228: *The end: Isn't it an eternal beginning?*

ABOUT THE AUTHOR

Verlaine-Diane Soobroydoo is a New York-based writer and community builder. She uses her life and words as vessels to build the positive change she wants to see. She is passionate about women's rights, social justice and personal development.

Unbound: Twitter thoughts for the heart and mind is her first collection of thoughts, poetry, and affirmations that have already reached over 500,000 people on Twitter. Her words engage on the power to conceptualize being in community with each other, and on the force of language to heal, help us self-transform, and reach liberation.

She is the founder of Zahara's Dream Inc., an impact initiative that builds positive change with and for young women worldwide.

Twitter: @VerlaineDiane // Verlaine-DianeSoobroydoo
www.instagram.com/verlainediane
www.verlainediane.com

ABOUT THE ILLUSTRATIONS

To bring an author's words to life with my illustrations, to be entrusted with such precious expression, always feels in high honor. It's about listening and reading 'between the lines' so to speak, so that I am able to visually dive deep into the meaning of what is being said. In the case of *Unbound*, I was drawn to the region from which Verlaine grew up, her home, her roots, which then bloomed the lilies that you see on the cover and throughout the book.

Many of the illustrations have been created to reflect my visual interpretation of Verlaine's words written on each page. I went with what came to my mind immediately after reading each line. Beginning this process of transferring my ideas to paper, the ideas for *Unbound* flowed so naturally as I dipped my brush pen into India ink and began the process of hand drawing each illustration.

I know they are a true representation of Verlaine's words but in so many ways they are a part of me as well. A reflection of what comes to mind when reading these powerful pieces that have shaped this most recent journey in the author's life. And knowing that to be the case made this experience of creativity that much more priceless, just as *Unbound* truly is.

Sarah Messina
@bysarahmessina

www.ingramcontent.com/pod-product-compliance
Lightning Source LLC
Chambersburg PA
CBHW072000110526
44592CB00012B/1161